rn ^{to be} Wild

# Little Elephants

## Anne Jonas

Words that appear in the glossary are printed in
**boldface** type the first time they occur in the text.

GARETH**STEVENS**
GS
PUBLISHING
A WRC Media Company

2

# A Loving Mother

A mother elephant never loses sight of her baby, or calf. If something frightens the elephants, she places her calf between her huge legs for protection, or she cuddles it with her trunk. Whenever she has to leave her calf, a mother finds another adult or an older sister to watch over it. What about the little elephant's father? He lives apart from the main **herd** of mothers and young elephants and never helps care for his young. Adult male elephants, or bulls, either live alone or with other bulls.

A female elephant gives birth to one calf every four years. When a calf is born, it is already a big baby. A newborn elephant stands 3 feet (1 meter) tall and weighs about 220 pounds (100 kilograms).

## What do you think?

How long does a female elephant carry her baby inside her body?

a) six months

b) a little over a year

c) almost two years

3

A female elephant carries her baby inside her body for almost two years.

When one of a herd's females, or cows, is about to give birth to a baby, the herd comes to a stop in the **savanna**. All the adults form a circle around the cow and turn their **tusks** toward the outside of the circle to protect her. Only one female stays next to the future mother to help her give birth. When the newborn calf can stand up on its legs, the other elephants leave their positions to admire it.

Just one hour after its birth, a little elephant can already walk. The calf's legs are shaking when it takes its first steps. Its mother uses her trunk to gently guide her baby.

Little elephants live with their mothers for a long time. When male elephants are about eleven years old, they leave the herd they grew up with. They are old enough to join a herd of adult males.

Elephant calves are very active. When a calf gets into mischief, its mother scolds it by clapping her ears against her head.

Although male elephants never take care of their young, they still keep an eye on the calves when they are nearby. They cut branches or pick up large amounts of grass for them.

# Grandma Is the Boss

Little elephants live with their mothers in a herd that includes between six and twenty females. All of the elephants in the herd obey the oldest female. She is the one who knows all the paths that lead to distant sources of water and the best pastures. She also knows if the herd should **flee** or fight in case of danger. When it is time for the herd to move, she gives the signal by raising her leg.

## What do you think?

What do elephants do when one of the herd is injured?

a) They stay with the injured animal and help it walk.

b) They bring it some food and then leave.

c) They **abandon** it and keep going on their way.

**When a herd is in danger, the elephants gather together. The young calves are placed in the middle, where they will be protected behind the adults' huge legs.**

Elephants care for and help each other. If one member of the herd gets hurt, the others will walk more slowly. They will even help the injured animal move by pushing it with their legs or trunks. When an elephant dies, its companions may cover its body with branches or dirt and stay with it for hours.

Elephants are the peaceful giants of the savanna and have only one enemy — people. Although it is illegal, people still hunt and kill elephants for their ivory tusks.

During a hunt, **poachers** try to kill the oldest female first. They know that the herd will become confused, frightened, and easier to capture.

8

The oldest female in the herd is extremely brave.
She attacks poachers to allow the other females
to flee with their calves.

# A Huge Appetite

A little elephant spends the first weeks of its life drinking its mother's milk. It is a real **glutton**. It drinks about 4 gallons (15 liters) a day, which is about the same as forty-five baby bottles of milk! As a calf drinks its mother's milk, it gently touches her belly with its trunk. Sometimes, the calf is fed by other females in the herd. Every female elephant produces milk throughout her entire adult life, which is very practical when it comes to feeding a group of hungry little elephants.

**Female elephants have two mammary glands located between their front legs. Although a calf can eat solid food at an early age, its mother will still feed it milk until the calf is about six or eight years old.**

What do elephants do when there is no more grass to eat?

a) They wait for new plants to grow.

b) They look for new pastures.

c) They start eating meat.

When there is no more grass to eat, elephants look for new pastures.

Elephants are the biggest **mammals** on Earth. They spend almost twenty hours a day eating grass, fruits, bark, branches, and even thorny bushes. In no time at all, an elephant herd can eat all the plants in its territory. They must constantly move to new pastures to keep feeding their big appetites.

When they are four months old, elephant calves start to eat mashed or ground up grass. They pick up the grass with their trunks.

Until a calf is one year old, it is small enough to walk between its mother's legs. When the calf is older and bigger, it will follow her everywhere.

Each day, elephants breathe in very fine soil and **sift** it through their mouths. The soil contains minerals that the elephants need to stay healthy.

What does an elephant do when the leaves on a tree are too high to reach? The elephant will eat the tree's bark instead, or it will simply knock the tree down to get to the leaves.

13

# Always Thirsty

When the savanna's heat and lack of rainfall turns the grass yellow and dries out the water holes, elephants become very thirsty. Like their parents, little elephants cannot survive many days without anything to drink. There is only one solution — the herd starts moving to find water, using the same paths that thirsty elephants have been using for centuries.

## What do you think?

Why do elephants take mud baths?

a) to change color and disguise themselves

b) to get rid of the bugs on their skin

c) to cover up their smell

Little elephants have not yet learned how to use their trunks to drink. Instead, the calves use their trunks like a kind of **snorkel** so they can breathe while drinking with their mouths.

## Elephants take mud baths to get rid of bugs on their skin.

Even though elephant skin is as thick as a human hand, it is very fragile. An elephant's skin is constantly irritated by the many insects that crawl or buzz over it. Elephants have an interesting way of getting rid of these pests. They take long mud baths! When it dries in the sun, the mud becomes a kind of shell that protects the elephants from the bugs.

There is nothing better for a calf than taking a long bath with some friends. A bath puts the calf in a good mood, especially when it can splash a few adults, too!

Elephants love taking dust baths. They scratch the ground with their feet, then suck up the dry soil with their trunks and blow it onto their bodies as if it were powder.

16

Elephants sometimes have difficulty finding water. They become so thirsty that they even try to find water that is hidden below the surface of the ground. They simply scratch the ground to get to the water.

When elephants find water, they rush to drink it. They suck up the water with their trunks, then spit it into their mouths.

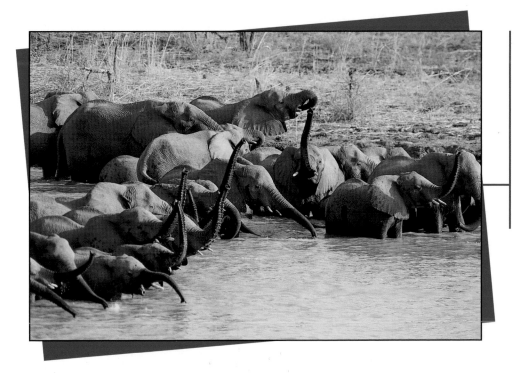

# Tricks of the Trunk

A little elephant does not know how to use its trunk yet, but it enjoys sucking on the end of it, just like a human baby sucks on its thumb. When a calf is about six months old, it will start using its trunk the same way the adults use theirs, and it will discover that its trunk is a marvelous tool. An elephant uses its trunk for drinking, showering, smelling, picking up seeds, knocking down trees, and even scratching the bottom of its ear.

An elephant trunk is one of a kind in the animal world. The trunk of an African elephant measures about 9 feet (3 m) long and looks like an arm with a two-fingered hand.

## What do you think?

How do elephants say hello to each other?

a) They shake their trunks.

b) They rub their ears.

c) They clatter their tusks.

## Elephants say hello to each other by shaking their trunks.

Elephants greet each other when they meet, even if they don't belong to the same herd. They touch, stroke, and sniff each other. Good manners require that the youngest elephants say "hello" first. By changing the position of its trunk, an elephant can express different feelings, such as curiosity, fear, or anger.

Elephants are usually peaceful animals, but they can become very angry. When they are angry, their tusks become dangerous weapons.

When an elephant wants to **reassure** or comfort one of its companions, it gently touches the other elephant with its trunk. If it wants to protect the other animal, it lays its trunk softly on its companion's head.

Elephants also use their trunks to hug each other. During mating season, a male elephant and a female elephant stay together for two or three days. They spend much of this time hugging each other with their trunks.

Elephants are mammals. African elephants live on the savannas of Africa. An adult African elephant weighs 4 to 7 tons (3.5 to 6 metric tons). Asian elephants live in the forests of India and southeast Asia. They are smaller than African elephants, and they have smaller ears and tusks and only one finger, instead of two, at the end of their trunks. In the wild, an elephant lives an average of sixty years.

Elephants are related to the tiny rock hyrax, the manatee, and the extinct mammoth.

Elephants grow all their lives. Males can reach a height of 13 feet (4 m).

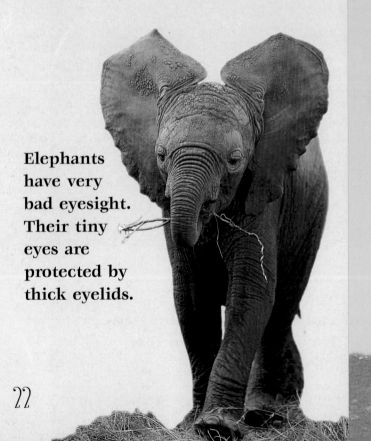

Elephants have very bad eyesight. Their tiny eyes are protected by thick eyelids.

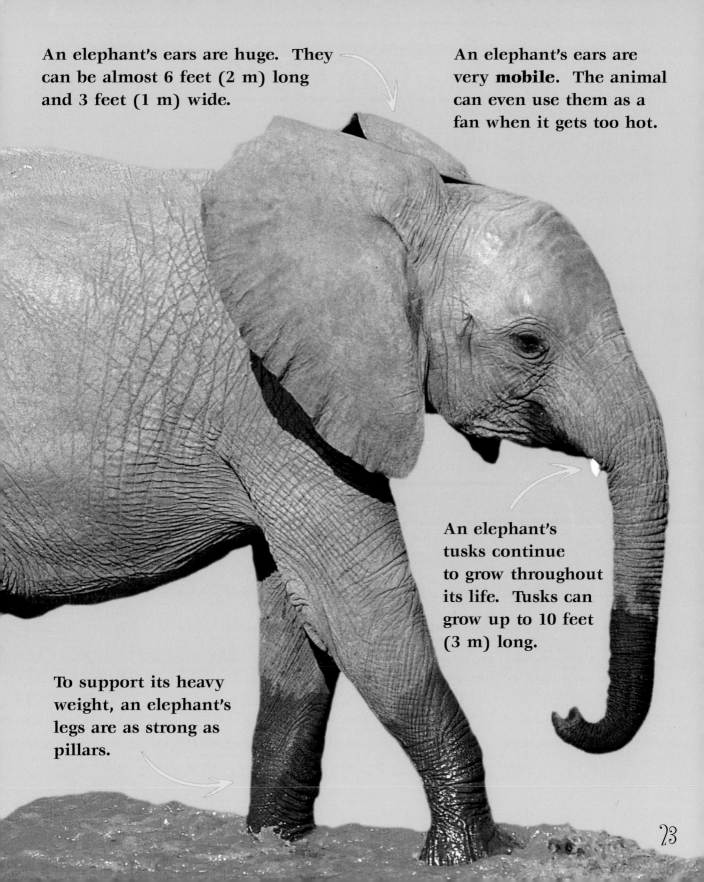

An elephant's ears are huge. They can be almost 6 feet (2 m) long and 3 feet (1 m) wide.

An elephant's ears are very **mobile**. The animal can even use them as a fan when it gets too hot.

An elephant's tusks continue to grow throughout its life. Tusks can grow up to 10 feet (3 m) long.

To support its heavy weight, an elephant's legs are as strong as pillars.

# GLOSSARY

**abandon** — to leave and stop giving support or help

**flee** — to run away from danger or trouble

**glutton** — someone who eats too much

**herd** — a group of one kind of animal that stays together

**mammals** — warm-blooded animals that have backbones, give birth to live babies, feed their young milk from the mother's body, and have skin that is usually covered with hair or fur

**mammary glands** — the parts of a female mammal's body that produce milk

**mobile** — capable of moving or being moved

**poachers** — people who kill or capture wild animals illegally

**reassure** — to make less afraid or worried; to restore confidence

**savanna** — a large, flat area of grassland with scattered trees, found in warm parts of the world

**sift** — to remove lumps from something by shaking or pushing it through a sieve

**snorkel** — a curved breathing tube used when swimming just under the surface of the water

**tusks** — huge, pointed teeth that stick out from the mouths of certain animals

Please visit our web site at: www.garethstevens.com
For a free color catalog describing Gareth Stevens Publishing's list of high-quality books and multimedia programs, call 1-800-542-2595 (USA) or 1-800-387-3178 (Canada). Gareth Stevens Publishing's fax: (414) 332-3567.

Library of Congress Cataloging-in-Publication Data

Jonas, Anne.
   [Petit éléphant. English]
   Little elephants / Anne Jonas. — North American ed.
      p. cm. — (Born to be wild)
    ISBN 0-8368-4434-3 (lib. bdg.)
   1. Elephants—Infancy—Juvenile literature. I. Title. II. Series.
QL737.P98J635   2005
599.67'139—dc22                    2004057442

This North American edition first published in 2005 by
**Gareth Stevens Publishing**
A WRC Media Company
330 West Olive Street, Suite 100
Milwaukee, Wisconsin 53212 USA

This U.S. edition copyright © 2005 by Gareth Stevens, Inc.
Original edition copyright © 2001 by Mango Jeunesse.

First published in 2001 as *Le petit éléphant* by Mango Jeunesse, an imprint of Editions Mango, Paris, France.

Picture Credits (t = top, b = bottom, l = left, r = right)
Bios: M. and C. Denis-Huot 3, 6, 14, 16(t), 18; M. Harvey/Fotonatura 2; M. Laboureur 5(t); G. Nicolet 17(b); M. Nicolotti 12(b), 20(b); C. Thouvenin 5(r). Colibri: C. Ratier 8(b); D. Haution 12(t), 23; P. Ricard 13(t). Jacana: Awup Shah cover, 10, 22; T. Davis 13(b). Phone: Jardel back cover; J.P. Ferrero/J.M. Labat title page, 4, 5(b), 7, 8(tl), 15, 16(b), 17(t), 19. Sunset: Weststock 9, Horizon Vision 20(t), 21.

English translation: Muriel Castille
Gareth Stevens editor: Barbara Kiely Miller
Gareth Stevens art direction: Tammy West

Printed in the United States of America

1 2 3 4 5 6 7 8 9 09 08 07 06 05